I JUST CAN'T STOP HERE

ADEREMI BADRU

Unless otherwise indicated, all scripture quotations are taken from the
King James Version

Printed in the United States of America
First Printing, 2019

ISBN : 978-1-908243-07-2

Published by :
The Base Media, UK.

For more information, contact :
Rev Aderemi Badru
bishopremibadru@gmail.com
remibadru44hope@yahoo.com
www.aderemibadru.org
Facebook: Aderemi Badru
Twitter: BishopBadru
Phone: 1-410-805-3016

Cover and Inner Design by:
CREATIVEGOSHEN
www.creativegoshen.com
+234-806-077-9227

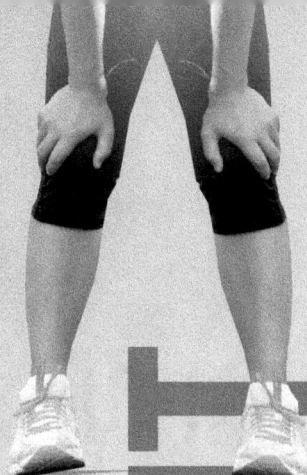

CONTENT

DEDICATION

This book is dedicated to my mentor and spiritual father, "Rev Akinyemi Hamid-Oke" who went home to be with the Lord on July 7th, 2018. You taught me to pay attention to details and to patiently follow the Lord wherever He leads me. You also showed me through your life that nothing can stop a man in the center of God's will. With each passing day, I can say that I am better as I reflect on everything you taught me and showed me. You were the first to read this material in 2012 but you wanted me to wait for the right time to publish this. Sleep on dear father! I miss you!

Aderemi Badru.
March, 2019.

ACKNOWLEDGEMENT

THANK YOU

The first time the Lord inspired me to write this book in 2012 was a moment of great uncertainty, transition and besetting trouble as I pursued to fulfill the call Of God on my life. Nevertheless, the Lord gave me strength, courage and capacity to write and to explain the things He has been teaching me through personal experiences and ultimately, the Scriptures. Therefore, I am eternally grateful to God who chose me as a voice of hope in this broken world. Furthermore, I am blessed with a beautiful and courageous woman who has constantly supported me and fought alongside me in pursuing God's purpose for our life. To her, I say thank you for providing me with such an enabling environment to write this material. Jesse David, Temitope Tremendous were the first set of people to edit the manuscript and I am grateful for your sacrifice. Barrister Femi Olugbemiro, thank you for editing this work professionally and for trusting in my unconventional style of writing.

I cannot but appreciate, Pastor Gary Smith (Bow Valley Baptist Church, Canada), Pastor Bukki Gbenro (TVC Ibadan, Oyo state, Nigeria) and Pastor Felix Makanjuola Jnr (RCCG Place of Victory, London) for prayerfully spending time to read through and contribute to this book. The silent role of Rev Tony Lawson in ensuring that I fulfil this work cannot be under-emphasized and I am so blessed to have such a great man that believes in God's call on my life. Finally, I am grateful to Adetayo Ayorinde (Director of Operations at CREATIVEGOSHEN) for arranging, designing and packaging this book excellently for God's glory. It is my earnest prayer that this book will become a tool in the hand of the Lord to encourage as many people who are at the verge of quitting on God's purpose for their lives.

Your Friend,
Aderemi Badru
April 2019.

READ THIS FIRST

Do you feel confused about what direction your life is going? Maybe you are at a crossroad and about to make a life changing decision or perhaps you are unsure about your career path. Until a man comes in alignment with destiny, he will forever wonder aimlessly in life. In this book, Rev. Badru carefully explores the subject of finding one's purpose and walking in it. Using biblical characters and contemporary examples, he has carefully laid out a road map to help anyone who may feel lost and distant from fulfilment. This is a good and practical read if you are ready to explore not just your potential but harness your God given destiny.

Pastor Felix Makanjuola Jnr
RCCG Place of Victory, Hackney, London. UK

Life is designed with the end in mind. Great people will always look ahead with the picture of their destination and never allow the rough terrain to deter them. The Author, did a great job to make this book a good compass for the journey of life. This book is very practical. Whoever pays attention to divine instructions in it will surely arrive at fair haven.

You will rest and then at the end of the days you will arise to receive what you have been allotted."

Bukki Gbenro
TVA, Inc. Nigeria

It is inspiring! I love it actually.

Garry Smith
Senior Pastor, Bow Valley Baptist Church, Calgary, Canada.

Brother Remi's personalized and direct style brings out the poignancy of this book. His in-depth understanding of the scriptures, his training and his personal experiences seeps through his writing and leaves a stark and indelible message on the heart of the reader. This book turns the heart of the reader towards God in a truly refreshing way...

Olufemi Olugbemiro Esq.
Paul Esther Consulting, Ohio, US.

Wow this is powerful!!!

No matter what the devil or others put in your way, never give up on God's purpose for you because God has not given up on you. It's not how you start your race, it's how you finish. Therefore run on for the victory lane is closer than you think!!!!!

Councilman Rev Tony Lawson
Senior Pastor, Damascus Road Baptist Church, Baltimore, Maryland

Your destiny is great and
if you do not fulfill it,
it will have a lot of damaging effects
on generations tied to your destiny.

1 A CHILD OF DESTINY

He was born at a time when the colonial masters were in charge of his community. They were so ruthless and callous in their dealings with the people that if any of their cars kill any child in the community, the parent must visit the owner of the car to say thank you. Nobody dared challenge them nor spoke up against their activities.

One of those days, as he was walking down the road with his sister, they got so engrossed and carried away in their discussion that they did not know when one of the colonial master's car was approaching, neither did they hear the horn of the car until the car came close to crushing them. Without hesitation, they jumped off the road into a pit, not knowing that a big cobra was in there.

Short of breath and words, they looked at each other with utmost hopelessness. How could this happen? They were running from death, but finally found themselves in this pit of death. Well, since there was nothing they could do, they were frozen in fear and resorted to accept whatever comes out of the situation. But, suddenly, the unexpected happened; the snake crawled out of the pit itself without hurting either of them.

They survived. As he shared this story with us, he recalled several incidents that followed this ordeal; how he took ill to the point of death and the several nightmares where he constantly saw snakes in his dream. All these were the results of the shock from the incidence. Yet , he survived the sickness. Today he is regarded as one of the greatest men on planet earth. Nevertheless each time he remembers that incident, it reminds him that he is a child of destiny.

My friend, this is one of the stories that Pastor E.A Adeboye shared with us and I want you to know that you are alive today is because you are a child of destiny.

How will you describe a child of destiny? What does destiny mean to you? What is the correlation between destiny and pre-destination? How do I discover my destiny? These are few out of numerous questions that people ask.

I am your creator and before you were born, I chose you to speak to the nations.

This is what the Al-mighty God wants you and me to know as He explains to Jeremiah in Jeremiah 1:2. Before you were born, God decided that you will be born without consulting anybody. It was solely His decision. Scientifically speaking, you were not the only sperm that tried, surviving to sought fertilization, but, you were the one God chose to mature. He decided everything about the coming together of your parents; where they met, how they met and even when you were conceived. I hope you have never thought that you are a product of an accident or a mistake?

Dear friends, it could not have been a coincidence that you survived the nine months in the womb, despite all the attacks your mother encountered during that period. It is even possible that you were born prematurely like me and no one could have believed that you have a chance of making it, yet you did. Do you still think it was a mere coincidence?

I know that you must have heard of many pregnancies that never led to child birth. Some were miscarried, some were aborted and some died at the time of delivery. Yet for you to be one of the few who has been given the privilege to live, then it should tell you that you are a child of destiny. Maybe this is one of the reasons why I don't believe in writing anyone off.

Everyone created by God is a child of destiny, although it is not all that will fulfill their respective destinies. So that you can understand the word destiny I need to call your attention to the word "destination".

Before you were born, **God took the decision for you to come but He also had a destination in mind (a MISSION He was sending you to the world for; an ASSIGNMENT you were coming to the world to accomplish; a PLAN you were to achieve and a SOLUTION you were to provide), that is why you were born and that is what is called DESTINY.**

He could have decided that you will not come to the world, but because you are part of His infinite plan. He chose to send you. I mean HIS PLAN. You and I never decided we wanted to come to this world. God decided it. We did nothing to come. He sent us. It was completely His choice and His decision how you were born, where you were born, and when you were born. All of this is because of the plan He conceived long ago.

He had a mission in mind when He was sending you into the

world so you were not just created to occupy space. This is what destiny is: *your destiny is what you were created by God to accomplish.* Simply put your reason for existence and your mission to the world. *If you don't fulfill that mission, you are simply a waste because that was why you were born.*

You must realize that it is not everyone that will fulfill their destiny, because the fall of man has led us to be rebels against God and ultimately man has been given the power of choice, which means that you can decide to comply with the plans of God for creating you and you may not. Hence, you must not forget that for every decision taken, there are always consequences.

This ability to choose is the reason a lot of people have decided to pursue their own ambition and desires. Consequently, when they stumble in such pursuits, they end up saying, "that is my own destiny". A lot of people like Adam are deceived to think that the plan God had for them when He sent them to the world is not great or wonderful. Therefore, they decide to seek what they call a 'better destiny'.

It is simply pathetic that what the enemy of man has succeeded in doing is to replace the desire to pursue the great destiny of each man with the lust of the flesh (FOOD), lust of the eye (WEALTH AND MATERIAL GAINS) and the pride of life (POWER). Whereas God has all these things already provided and packaged for our survival. We often fail to realize that our creator will not send us on an assignment at our own expense.

It was before Adam was created that He created the Garden of Eden and inside the garden were all that Adam needed for living. In His own benevolence, He saw that Adam would need a companion, so provided Eve for Him. Why then will that kind of a father send you and me to this world to accomplish a purpose for Him and abandon us? This is what so many people don't know which has turned them to slaves who can do anything for food, for wealth, power, and worldly pleasure.

What a deceit! Your destiny is not just to eat, drink, wear clothes, build houses, buy cars and bear titles. You are on a mission that God planned a long time before you were born and all those things are already provided in the package that will make the mission possible.

It is pathetic that many people have no desire to even find out who God really calls them or the purpose for which He sent them to the world. However, they have been manipulated to believe that living a fulfilled life is all about the cars you buy, how rich you are, the houses you build, the degrees you have, the children you have, the places you have been to, and ultimately the wealth you were able to amass for yourself.

Friends, there is more to life than those things. Jesus our Lord in his sermon on the mount warned us about the anxiety for what to eat, drink and what to wear. He asked a question that you and I should pay attention to; He said, "is not the life more than meat and the body more than raiment? Matthew 6:25b". Our purpose is beyond those things because the truth is that you were not made for yourself, but you were made by God for His purpose and pleasure. Until we get to understand this truth, we will not be free from worrying, anxiety, and fear because these things are the things that God gives at will to anyone He choose to. He owns them and that is just the truth. I am always excited to remind people that God said that He is the one that gives seed to the planter and bread to the eater.

Many people have lived and died without even finding out the reason for their existence. The devil is always happy with such people because he knows they pose no threat to him. As long as you don't have an idea of why you were born and you think that all you were born to do is for yourself then the devil rejoices each time he sees you.

I hope you know that the devil has always been afraid of man since when God placed all things under man's dominion. By the standards of creation both by mode and structure, he should be superior to man yet God made man out of dust and placed all things under him. Is that not why the devil will never allow anyone to discover his true identity and destiny until he or she is dead? Similarly the devil keeps using what belongs to you and later come to tell you if you bow to me I will give them to you. Were they not yours in the first place? Are they His?

Can you imagine that when the LORD came to the world in the form of a man, the devil came to him with these same temptations to dissuade him out of his purpose and destiny? He failed because the Lord had the knowledge of who He was and what He had. **The devil is always going about replacing glorious destinies with empty pursuits.** That is why people that were made to save their generation are occupied with saving their stomach only. There are millions of people who were sent to the world to restore good leadership and save the world's economy. Where are they? They are busy pursuing how to survive.

I believe that it is time for you to know that God did not create us to buy cars, build houses, have children, possess degrees and make money. Those things are lesser things and cannot be compared to the beauty of your destiny. You are on earth to fulfill a mission that God created you for.

The question you should be asking yourself is, 'What is my mission on earth'. In fact, your parents ought to have asked God on your behalf since you were in the womb and they were supposed to direct you in that area when you were born. However many of the parent don't even know that there is more to living than mere surviving. Some of them have also been helping the devil in misleading their children out of God's purpose for their lives. If many of them never even know the reason for their own existence, how will they search their children's? As I read through the scriptures, I noticed that before children were born, God will reveal who the child is, what the child will be and do when he comes to the world so it was easy for these children to pursue their destinies.

God did not create more than six billion people to occupy space or gather wealth. **He gave each one of us a unique assignment with unique potentials and gifts; as a result, we are all different from each other.** The controversies of competition ought not to exist among us if understand who we are and what God has made us for. **No man born of a woman is born without a divine mandate.** Isaac was born for a purpose, in the same way God allowed the birth of Ishmael for a purpose. When Haggai was running away from Sarah, the angel of the Lord met him and called the child a great child. Someone could have asked, why are you calling this child great? A child that was born out of wedlock, rejected, and unwanted? What is great about him? But the one that made him said "He is a great child". Why? He sent him to the world for a purpose. What I may not know is if they fulfill their destiny or not.

Have you discovered your destiny? One thing about the greatness of God is that in His wisdom, He has done all things perfectly; He has gifted all of us unique destiny. What becomes of your destiny is solely your responsibility but you are a child of destiny.

Some people have tried to explain that we have a universal purpose which is to bring praise to God through everything that we do, but there is also a specific purpose for creating each one of us. Some were created as builders, some as beautifiers, some as doctors, some as masons, some as entertainers and much more but in all, we were all made to serve His purpose. As we serve His purpose, we will be displacing the enemy and taking over the kingdom of this earth for God. We are to establish the kingdom of God on earth.

As I read the Bible, I discovered that God had a plan for Jacob just like he had for Esau, but their parents almost destroyed them foolishly.

When Jacob got married and his wife Rachel was barren, she never knew that during that period God was preparing a savior from and for their family. God knew ahead that in their journey that there would be a severe famine and someone will need to go ahead of them to Egypt to save them from the famine when the time comes.

Imagine if Joseph had not fulfilled his destiny, then the family would have died of famine. **Your destiny is great and if you do not fulfill it, it will have a lot of damaging effects on those generations tied to your destiny.**

I have heard several people talk about God having favorites, but in my little understanding, **I discovered that this uncreated CREATOR has never made a mistake.** When he made Joseph, and brought him to a family where he was hated, someone could have asked, why? He also allowed the mother to leave him at a tender age, but that was also not a mistake. When the brothers sold him to Egypt, it might look like wickedness but that was not a mistake. But Joseph never knew that the early understanding of God's plan kept him moving until he got to a place of fufilment.

Everything will be dark and confusing to you until you realize that you are a child of destiny. You may have even failed in several attempts you made on some pursuits in life. There might even be painful and sad experiences you are going through now, yet all of those things will be of great advantage to you later, if you stick to the plan God has for you when you were born. I want you to take time to find out what your purpose is because that is the only way for you to become all you were made to be.

God is not partial. He did not make the whites better than the blacks nor the blacks better than the whites. He did not make the short inferior to the tall or the tall inferior to the short. He has never made a mistake. He decided that you should be born where you are and the way you are. A lot of people have tried to change who they are because they felt others were better than them. You are just the best of your kind, what is important is for you to discover your destiny and fulfill it.

Just for a moment, pause and ask why God has preserved you? Do you think that you were created to live for yourself? No, your existence is more than you. Your life is not for you; it is for the one that made you. It is when a man is living according to the will and plan of his creator that we can say he is fulfilling destiny. Consider Moses, his birth speaks volume about him. He was born at a time when it was prohibited for the Jews to have male children. In fact, all the male children that were given birth to at that time were killed but that was the time that God had planned for Moses to come precisely to Egypt.

Moses was born when his parents were under affliction and

great suffering because God had chosen him and ordained him as a deliverer to his people. That was why all the attempts to kill him failed. It is important for you to know that children of destiny don't die anyhow especially when they have committed their lives to pursuing their God given destiny. A useful and fruitful tree is not cut down anyhow because it is serving its purpose. The Lord Jesus made it clear that any tree that does not bear fruit will be cut down and thrown into the fire. My friends, I know that God will do all He can to protect any child of destiny. You must realize that your destiny is your security. Although you will be attacked, you will come out of the fire shining.

Moses at his encounter with God saw a bush that was on fire but that was not consumed which is an illustration of two things to him: first, to show him that he has gone through fire and has not been consumed because he is a child of destiny. Second, to show him that the children of Israel his people have been in fire and they will not be consumed because God loves them and that He has chosen him to rescue them from that fire.

Friends, I call you to ponder on why God has not allowed your errors to destroy you like Moses. Think about why God has preserved you through the fire you have gone through. Is it not because of your destiny? Do you know why everything seems to be working against you? Is it not because the devil is aware of how great your destiny is?

You must realize that as a child of destiny, you are both special to God and a special target to the devil. You are a child of destiny; God has a destination in mind for you before sending you into the world.

As I conclude this chapter, let me point it out to you that you are an influence maker, a world changer and you were created to show forth the glory of your God. All of us were made by Him and for Him. This is why our destinies will never be fulfilled until we discover his plans and purpose for our lives. Those that live for Him often die happy and even in death their memories are blessed. But those that live for themselves often die wretched and poor. Jesus asked His disciples and He is asking you also, "is life not more than food, the body, and raiment?". Your destiny is more than mere surviving and those frivolities, it is to glorify your Maker and to fulfill the mission that he sent you to the world for. He has plans to give you all you need to live godly and enjoy your days. He has never sent a soldier to battle without adequate provision.

On the 21st of October, 2011, I was involved in a ghastly motor accident with four of my children on our way back from a crucial meeting that has to do with our destiny. The car somersaulted and got wrecked but the five of us came out alive. There and then some of the people that came to rescue us said these people must be special to God, and they agreed that we were kept by a divine power. I asked God "why?" and He said, " I kept you for myself and to fulfill the assignment I sent you to the world for". Therefore, each time I wake up I keep telling Him that I want my whole life to be an expression of His grace. When you live for the one that created you and for the purpose for which He created you, then He will constantly watch over you to perform His word in your life. Majoring on the minors of life will cut your life short. God loves you and that is why He chose you to come to the world, why not find out why He sent you?

Of a truth, you are just wasting
your time and energy if
your life is not in accordance
with the purpose for which
God created you.

2. SHOW ME MY DESTINY!

He was just sixteen years old, loved by his father, hated by his siblings yet he kept dreaming. He dreamt of how his bundle stood up while that of his brothers gathered around his own and bowed to it. His brothers could not understand his dreams so they stored up hatred in their heart towards him. Few days later, he had another dream and told his father in the presence of his brothers that he saw eleven stars, moon and sun bowed to him. This aroused more envy and jealousy towards him until they thought, planned and concluded that the best thing to do was to kill or sell him. Why? He caught a glimpse of what the plan of God for his life is.

Friends, I have come to discover that until you know God's plan for your life; until you know your destination and you can say this is where God is taking me to, you will continue to live in frustration, anger, and jealousy of those around you who can say boldly that this is where God is taking me to. One of the reasons that there is so much unhealthy competition and rivalry among us is because we often feel that those that have discovered the purpose of God for their lives act as if they are better than those who are yet to have an idea of where there are going in life.

Of a truth, you are just wasting your time and energy if your life is not in accordance with the purpose for which God created you. In fact, you will spend your life in frustration and anger because you will be living a borrowed life or working in another person's field. I believe until you know God's plan for your life, every other thing you know is useless. Don't you think that it will be foolish for you to embark on a journey when you don't have a destination in mind? Yet I see several of us live life without knowing anything about our destiny. Of course, what is the value of your existence, when you don't know your mission on earth not to talk of pursuing it? The discovering of your destiny is more important than all the education you can ever acquire. Your knowledge of why you were born is important than having all the knowledge of this world.

In view of this, you can be sure the devil will do anything he can to hide your purpose in life from you and will want to replace your purpose with other pursuits. ***Do you know who you are? Why God created you the way you are? Why He sent you to this part of the world and other thought-provoking questions are questions you must find answers to. Until you find answers to those questions, I suggest that you pause for a while and don't just continue travelling to an unknown destination.*** Our Lord and Savior Jesus Christ got to that point when He had to define his purpose; he said 'for this cause was I born'.

John the Baptist's mission was clearly stated before his birth, the same with Samson. In the days of old, parents were more concerned with knowing who their children will be and what God has destined for them but today parents are more concerned with choosing their children's path for them and forcing them to follow it. But, if you check why they do such, you will discover that it is for their own personal gain and benefit. They are less concerned about if the children are fulfilling destiny or not.

You must realize that you were not created to fulfill your parents' dreams or what your friends wants you to be. The society we live in have a way of placing demands on our lives but you are the one that will seek to discover who you really are. A lot of people on this planet earth are living a

borrowed life. My friends, you are on a mission to this world, the same way your parents, siblings, and friends on their respective missions too. But many of those we are surrounded with do not care about that mission as long as they have what to eat or drink.

Friends, I am not inviting you to be religious but to stop wasting your life. God has an agenda for your life with a time allotted for you to fulfill it, a location for you to fulfill it and how you will go about it. Since He is our manufacturer, He has in His hands the manual about each one of us. We are not created to live anyhow, but to live for our maker and fulfill His purpose for sending you. **If you have not discovered your purpose and mission to this world, it means you are either living a wasted life or living a borrowed life.**

God did not create you to just attend church and be religious but to affect your world positively. What is the value of being a child of God when you are not shining your light in the midst of darkness? Fulfilling your destiny is what matters not just attending church. The church is supposed to help you know God, His purpose for your life, and empower you to fulfill it not just to cage you in religious activities. God created Adam to establish His kingdom on earth but the devil distracted him. Eventually, God sent Jesus to save us so that we might re-establish His purpose for sending us. Hence as our God is concerned about us fulfilling our mandate, we are more concerned about survival and pursuing our selfish ambition.

It is time for us to realize that the Lord did not create us just to make a living (survivals) but as saviors to save our generation from the enemy and that is why He loaded each of us with unique and great potentials, gifts and talents. **Every one of us is anointed to solve a problem.** To be anointed is to be set apart and if you understand that, it means you are set apart by God in the unique physique He gave you to be a problem solver in your generation. While we focus on obtaining a good degree that will earn us a good living, we have forgotten our destiny, the agenda of the one that made us in His image. Our prayers only reflect our ambitions and not a passion to fulfill destiny but the question remains how shall we fulfill the destiny we know not?

Our prayers and earnest desires should be that God the manufacturer of us all will reveal to us His intents and purpose for making each one of us so that we will not end up regretting at the end. Only few of us are really praying for what we should pray for. A lot of us live our lives in fear of death because we cannot boast of living a purposeful or a meaningful life. Yes, death does not scare men and women of purpose because they are living for a greater cause and they know that until they fulfill that cause they cannot die. Perhaps I should ask you my reader, if you will be willing to cut down a fruitful tree? Won't you rather be looking for a way to keep the tree healthy so that it can produce more fruits? The gardener is under compulsion to take care of a fruitful garden and protect it against all harms, why then should you and I be living in fear of death and evil if we are truly fulfilling the purpose of our creator?

Religion has blinded our eyes to the truth and each time I see the crowd gathering in the different worship centers, I ask myself why they have gathered. They have gathered so that God can give them food and protect them so that they can continue to live for their own pleasure and passion. It is high time we sought to know the real purpose of our existence. We must stop living for our self and start fulfilling destiny. We must be awakened to the truth that we are just wasting away if all that we live for is what we will eat or drink. I wish you can cry out to God that He might show you your destiny. What is the will of God for your life? The answer to that question should be your motivation for life. What is it that you really want from life? Mediocre think about themselves alone and what they can possess but giants think of living a fulfilled life; the kind of life that will affect the world positively and that can bear heaven's attestation. What do you want?

Among different parables that Jesus shared with His disciples when He was on earth, is the story of the profitable servant. That story continues to inspire me every day to know and always bear in mind that the master has given to everyone different assignments with different talents according to our abilities. No one was considered useless. The one that had five talents is as important as the one that had one. But why the others were carrying out their assignments, the one that had one felt cheated. I can imagine how he looked at the other servants with hot jealousy not knowing that they were not the one that choose what they were given but the master. Everyone was given talents and assignments as it pleased the master which is perfectly in according to His plan.

How I wish all of us will realize the uniqueness of our destiny? God that created us all without consulting anyone created us with a unique plan and assignment which is why none of us was created as a photocopy of anyone. He did that to fulfill His own plan. He gave us gifts and potentials needed to finish our assignments here on earth. We were sent here to accomplish different things but ultimately to make the earth HIS THRONE.

I sat down recently pondering on what could have happened to the world if God had made us all to be the same and given us all the same assignment. If He made all of us as doctors, who will be the accountants, the carpenters, the masons, the lawyers and teachers? Hence, the fact that He sent some to be lawyers, some to be masons, fashion designers, musicians and so on; that in any way does not make anyone inferior to others or superior. This is the wisdom of the ALL-KNOWING CREATOR.

The Almighty God who knows the end from the beginning desires that all of us will live and stick to the purpose for which He made us. He does not want us to deviate or be distracted but how can we pursue a course we know nothing about? People have asked severally, how to know the plan God has for them and His purpose for me and I have simply responded by asking them to ask their maker themselves. What any motivational speaker will tell you about your destiny is not as important as what your maker tells you Himself. He is the one that conceived you in His thought before forming you and sending you to the world. He knows everything about you before you were born because you are the product of His thought and decision.

Your parents were supposed to guide you and help you to know God, so that He can reveal His purpose and plan for your destiny, but since many of our parents never came to know God's purpose for their own lives; how then will they be able to guide their children? Fulfilling your destiny is more important and crucial than becoming what your parents want you to be. Let me re-emphasize this that YOUR DESTINY is what GOD CREATED YOU TO BE and it implies FULFILLING THE MISSION FOR WHICH HE SENT YOU TO THE WORLD FOR; anything short, makes you a waste, irrespective of your achievement.

Myles Munroe in his book *"In Pursuit of Purpose"* made it clear that it is not everyone that died that lived. The cemetery is filled with people who were buried with their potentials, gifts and talents. There lies men and women who never fulfilled destiny. While several of them thought they have excuses and genuine reasons they can give to God that made them not to fulfill the purpose for which He sent them to the world, but many will be amazed and surprised to know at the end, that God gave them more than enough opportunities to discover their destiny and fulfill it. The sad part of this issue is that some people discovered what they were sent the world to do when their time was up.

Friends, what is the value of a tree that refuses to bear fruits? What is the use of laboring on a garden that will not produce any crop? Don't you think that some people were taken away by God after He has labored over them and had given them chances to fulfill the purpose, for which He made them, yet they were fruitless and some of them were producing bad fruits? Is He not justified if He decides to take away such people?

The Lord Jesus in one the parables He used to illustrate kingdom truths and principles to His disciples told us of a gardener who spent so much strength and invested; so much resource in growing a tree. Hence at the time when he was supposed to find fruits on the tree could not find any. Year in year out, this gardener kept coming to see if he will find any fruit but was always disappointed. That did not make him abandon the tree but he kept taking care of it, hoping that it will soon become fruitful. However, he got tired of wasting all he had on the tree. Do you remember that the conclusion of the owner was to cut the tree down? At the end, he said "why should it continue to use up my space and strength"? So, he decided to cut it down. Does that not illustrate many of us that have not been useful and productive to the one that made us? Yet He has continued to lavish us with His grace and love. Will He not be justified if He decided to take us away? This is one mystery about death that I wish you pay attention to!

Although the servants of the owner pleaded with him to give the tree one more year after which it can be chopped down if it remains fruitless; that explains the grace and love that many of us have enjoyed over the years. But it is sad to note that so many people are living out their last year (chance) after God had given them enough opportunities to fulfill destiny and be productive. What will you do if God were to reveal to you that you are living in your last chance and anytime soon, he will not hesitate to cut you down? Friends, anyone who is not fulfilling destiny and fruitful is as good as dead because it is just a matter of time that the owner will come and uproot and replace the tree. My question to you as you read this book remains; what are you living for? Are you sure that you are fruitful and productive? Is your creator happy with you? I hope He is not already concluded on uprooting you? You must find true answers to those questions and until you can, you better stop chasing shadows.

In addition, there was also an occasion that the Lord Jesus was hungry in one of His numerous outings and as He approached a particular tree, which He was expecting to find fruits, but He was disappointed to discover that there was no fruit on the tree. He then went on to place a curse of the tree; if you ask me, why the Lord will go to the extent of cursing the tree, I will tell you that I believe He wanted to make the disciples clearly understand how the creator feels each time He comes to see His children. When He sees fruits, He pronounce more blessings but when He does not He becomes angry and instead of blessings, the fruitless tree becomes cursed.

A fruitless tree is useless to the gardener and in the same vein anyone who is not fulfilling destiny is a waste to His maker. How I wish you understand the implications of not living according to the purpose and plan of God for your life? I wish you know how angry and sad God becomes when after all His investments on our lives, we remain fruitless and unproductive?

My friends, God hates barrenness, purposelessness, and wastage. Of a truth what He seeks from us every day is if we are living the life, He created us to live; He wants to see us fulfill the purpose for which He made us and anything short of that makes us a waste to Him. He can do anything to keep us, protect us and provide for us but until we are bringing pleasure to Him, we are breaking His hearts and the only way to bring pleasure to Him is by daily living for Him and for the purpose for which He made us. Do you now know why you must not rest until you have a thorough understanding of your destiny?

It is very crucial for you to pay attention to the discovery of your destiny because that is what determines everything about you. It is your purpose (mission in life) that determines who you will marry, where you will live, your companions and that you will do. So many people have married the helper of someone else's destiny since they have no idea of what their own purpose is. In fact, let me submit here that it is not appropriate for a man who has not discovered his purpose to think of marriage because the wife will end up in frustration and will eventually become lost. Permit me to break the word RELATIONSHIP into two; RELATIONS and SHIP. What this connotes is that two people in a RELATIONSHIP must be RELATED and they must be on the SAME SHIP going to the SAME PLACE. The two of them must be born of God to enjoy a blissful relationship, which means they are related and must be on the journey to the same destiny.

Why there is so much confusion and pain in so many marriages is because the husband and the wife often are not related and are not going to the same place. The husband has a different agenda and so is the wife. But, it is most pathetic for a lady to join herself with a man who does not have an idea of where he is going but is just travelling to any direction. It is the understanding of that destination that gives a sense of direction in everything. If a man who is sent to Asia as the light of their economy ends up with a woman who was made to help a certain man sent to Africa to change their political system; then tell me why that marriage will not fail? The first issue to be sorted out is why were you born? You must sit with God to know what He sent you to the world to do because that is what gives direction to everything you do in life. I hope you have truly started living? Because you have not started living until you can boldly say 'for this cause was I born!'

In my journey here on earth I have met several people whose pursuits in life is as a result of what people say about them. Some of them are who they are today because of what their parents said about them or their friends or even their enemies. They have never for once sat down to know what God really said about them. They are so comfortable with the achievements and what men call success that they do not care what God really says. They have not come to realize that there is a vast difference between fulfillment and achievement. If a man that was born to be a teacher becomes a doctor and becomes very rich in terms of possessions and wealth, what we see of him is a great man but what God sees about him is someone that is wasting away. Consequently, when he returns to God he will not be asked of how much wealth he acquired but if he fulfilled the purpose for which he was sent to the world. Pursue to fulfill destiny and your joy will know no bounds when you return to your maker.

The recent trend in the society is the lust for success at all cost. Many will kill and do all manner of things to be considered successful but my question remains; what is success? When I was in the seminary, in one of our discussions in the Christian Philosophy class, we were taught that there is a vast difference between appearance and reality. It is possible for us to see a man's appearance and conclude that he is successful but in the real sense the life of that person has no worth. How a man looks does not reflect success because we will be foolish to judge a book by its cover. Many of the so-called celebrities have died in frustration when they discovered how empty and meaningless their lives have been despite their so-called success.

Power, fame, money, and sex that they had could not replace the satisfaction they ought to have from living a fulfilled life. Many of them looked rich but die poor. It is time for us to sit and consider what truly gives a man satisfaction. Success is not having possession of great wealth or living a long life but it is accomplishing the purpose for which life was giving to us.

As I was growing up, I took a decision that I would rather die poor and live a fulfilled life than becoming rich and live a wasted life. My sincere desire is that you pay attention to the discovering of why you were created before you will continue pursuing shadows. Don't deceive yourself because you will end up regretting you did; you must find out why God created you and sent you to the world at a time like this. The manual always comes with the product and since you are God's product, that means the manual of your life is in God's hand and only Him can tell you what is in it. No matter what anyone tells you about who you are, it is irrelevant until you hear from your maker yourself. You must ask Him 'show me my destiny!' I can't forget when He told me that I was born to bring His people back to Him, to His plan and purpose for their lives and to rebuild the broken, wounded and the shattered ones.

My friends, it was this discovery that changed me, that led me thus far, that guided me in the choice of every step I have taken thus far and that has kept me going. I may not yet be all that He told me or have reached the destiny He showed me, but I take each step daily in the pursuit of that great destiny and I know I will get there someday. Have you discovered your destiny? Do you know where you are going? If no, stop now and ask the only one that knows your end from the beginning!

No one wants to go through
the fire but that is the only path
for gold to become gold

We must not give up now no matter
how hard the path to that destiny maybe.

3 CONFUSED AND LOST ...

29th of November, 1999 remains a memorable day in my life because that was when my destiny began to unfold. It was not long after I had finished my secondary school with great aspirations, dreams and ambitions to become the Governor of Central Bank of my great country Nigeria and later become the president of my country. I can still recall vividly how I inscribed this dream on my cupboard in school and on the walls of my room. Some of my friends and my mother used to call me PRESIDENT ADEREMI BADRU.

I was so passionate about this dream that I kept telling everyone around me. When I graduated from the secondary school, I was admitted into a tertiary institution precisely Osun state polytechnic Iree, but I rejected the offer because the admission was to study a course that has nothing to do with my ambition. I was willing to wait until I could gain admission to any institution that will offer me the course that I wanted so that I can become what I wanted to be. This was a great dream to my parents, teachers and friends but no one ever told me that I was born for a purpose. According to the error of the human heart that often forgets God and His plans, but tends to follow the path that seems to have greater personal gain and benefits, I went on pursuing this dream.

Divine interruption is what I called what happened to me on that fateful day. As I was busy with the house chores, the Lord said to me "go inside I want to speak to you". I went inside and sat and was waiting for what He will say. Few minutes later, **I heard Him say "Aderemi, my people are suffering, my church is defiled and has lost the passion for which I died for the world. The rate at which the devil is destroying and enslaving my people is alarming and I have raised you to restore my people, to rebuild the broken walls of my church, to release my people from their slavery, and to reform the standard of righteousness in your generation."** Oh, I could not eat nor drink for days as the burden of what the Lord showed me consumed me.

I never knew that what the Lord told me will in turn change the course of my pursuits in life. A day after the encounter, a friend came and shared with me the same instructions that God gave him concerning me. I became sadder and I could not hide asking God why He decided to choose me. I reminded him of my background and my ambitions in life but He kept telling me "that was why I was born". I tried resisting but when I could not resist further. I was so curious to know what was next and whether all these would come to pass. Oh! I was ready but foolishly thought the vision will be fulfilled immediately.

After I received this revelation, I went to meet my pastor and told him I was ready to run with the vision that God had shown me. He smiled at me and told me that the vision is for an appointed time and that God will equip me for the task before sending me. I got angry with him because I was just expecting him to approve it and announce to the church that my son is now a minister of God, but I never knew that there is a process I must go through. I continued to seek answers to my questions but I was shocked when the Lord told me to prepare myself to study at the federal Polytechnic Ede, Osun state, Nigeria.

I wondered why God would want me to be His servant and still ask me to go and study in Ede but I obeyed Him and sought admission at the school. I knew God really wanted me to be at that school because the Deputy Rector who was my Uncle told me that the school cannot be admitted because I lacked one of the basic requirements to study the course I wanted to study but as I got back home the Lord told me that I will get the admission and it happened like that. I was surprised when I was called that I have been given admission to study in three different departments, so I resumed. I remember vividly as a student, the first person I ever met on that campus, when I asked her for direction replied by calling me 'pastor sir', so I wondered where I knew her or whoever told her that I was called of God. However, that was how God started training me. It soon became very clear why God wanted me to go there to study. There I made mistakes, learnt obedience and was taught the power of humility. I did not know how proud and arrogant I was until the Lord began to show me how the devil was scheming to destroy my destiny through anxiety and worry over my marital relationship. God really dealt with my appetite and made me realize that He wanted me to be was His son and friend much more than being a pastor.

Three years later, as I was rounding off my program, I heard the Lord said to me "prepare for the next phase of your training at the seminary". On hearing that, I was so angry with myself because I was one of those people that believed that the seminary is a cemetery and I had also preached that in a message. I felt the empowerment from God is what I needed and not education but I did not argue because I had already decided to always obey Him and never to have any ambition of my own but to always submit to the will of God in all things. I told my friends that I was ready to go to the seminary; many of them felt that I was insane to have taken such a decision. I remembered my sponsor in school decided not to have anything to do with me again if I leave school and go to the seminary. But as much as I had no funds to go, I must obey the Lord.

Therefore, in August 2004 I resumed at the Nigerian Baptist Theological Seminary Ogbomosho for the next phase of my preparation for destiny. What will I say about my experience at the seminary? It was a very painful, bitter and a hard one. Several times I attempted to leave but God sent people like the late Dr. S. Ola Fadeji to show me that where He was taking me to was greater than what I was going through. I was misunderstood by several people around me. I could not relate with the pattern of doing things in the seminary. I had visions that were burning in me, yet I was loaded with academic responsibilities.

I also kept falling sick and because I was so much engrossed in the work of ministry even as a student. I started stepping on toes. Effort to settle down in relationship did not work and I was faced with several accusations, yet I kept wondering why God will take me to such a school. At some points, I noticed that I was odd in the school and I was being supervised right, left and center by people who were looking for an opportunity to discredit my ministry and crucify me.

In year 2006, God spoke to me about church planting in LAUTECH Ogbomoso and I shared that with my great friend and mentor in school but I could also notice that he was already getting tired of me with several controversies that surrounded me. But the church soon started and in another dimension the Lord started teaching me new things. As the church kept growing, the training continued both at the school and at the church. But, I soon realized the error of trusting people and not seeking the Lord before bringing people close to myself. That lesson took me away from where I loved to be to where I do not want to be.

As graduation was drawing near, my fiancé and I decided to seek the Lord for further instructions on the next step for the ministry after my seminary training and the Lord made it clear to us that we should get ready to go to Abuja for the next phase of our training but He will tell us when to leave. We related this to the church that called us to serve and at the long run we were sent to Abuja to pioneer a church. I never knew that the training in Abuja will be that difficult, I thought it will be sweet and tantalizing. There were times we were hungry and, could not afford meals and good clothing for my wife yet, the new-baby church must not suffer. We started running from pillar to post, to different people and churches to ensure that the church survives and we can also survive. This in turn made us look like 'beggars' to so many people. I remember that a pastor once told one of his members that they should not attend to me if I ask them for support because I have insatiable needs.

Several times, my wife and I got tired, frustrated, discouraged and were practically left alone with no one to encourage us. At a point, I said to myself that this is not the dream and vision that God showed me. Why will God show me a great future and I will be going through such frustrating experiences. The vision of a glorious destiny that I saw practically looked impossible. My boss was not even helping matters as he was practically frustrating us and we were turned out by almost everyone around us. I could not but notice the frustration on my wife's face and we felt lost and completely shattered. The churches and their pastors that surrounded us were also against us because they felt we had come to compete with them and we kept wondering what God was actually doing to us. At a point I felt like asking God why He did not allow me to remain an accountant but called me to the ministry and now I could not feed my family nor fulfill my dreams for the ministry.

Nevertheless, before we get to any breaking point, God would send help to us. At a point we told the Lord that we needed a car and He told us that He had a plan but we were in a hurry to get one so we pushed ourselves into serious trouble that we realized late. As all these went on and as the year 2011 began, we heard the Lord say "now is the time for you to leave Abuja and start your ministry." I quickly asked the Lord why He wanted us to leave at a time when we had nothing on us; a time we could not afford to feed ourselves; a time we didn't have accommodation; and a time we had people turning against us and calling us fools. These questions were on our lips as we did not know what to say to the Lord. I was so scared to break the news to my wife, not knowing that the Lord had already spoken to her. How then are we going to move? Where we were going to and how we will survive there were answers I needed to provide for my wife to prove that I was convinced of Gods instruction.. It was at that juncture that I realized that the whole time we spent in Abuja was for us to learn how to trust God and obey Him. Does that sound well to you? To me, it did not because humanly speaking the step we were about to take looked like a suicide mission; yet God considered it as the next step to be taken to fulfill destiny.

Friends, I know you wonder why I am sharing this long story with you. This is just to give you an illustration that will help you understand that the path to the destiny God showed to you is not smooth. As I meditated on the path that the lord had taken us through, I heard him say" DESTINY CAN'T STOP HERE; of a truth you are going through a hard time and it is difficult for you to see pass what you see right now. I know that you are even finding it difficult to see a ray of light in this darkness that surrounds you but I still hear God says "destiny can't stop here" what you must know is that God can't deceive you about what he showed you and what you are going through now is just a part.

I know we are not the only one that is fully lost and confused. It is possible that of a truth, you know that you are a child of destiny and you have everything it takes to fulfill the destiny. Right now, you are tired, confused, frustrated, discouraged, weak, and almost lost. I feel your pains and you should know the savior passed through the reforming fire. God did not tell Joseph that he was going to be hated by his brothers; he did not tell him that he would be sold; he never mentioned it to him in his dream that he will become a slave in the Potiphar's house; nor did God pre-inform him that he will be thrown into the prison. Nonetheless, he had to follow that path to fulfill destiny. It is possible that you have decided to give up because of what you are going through. You must realize that every child of destiny must follow the Lord through the path that leads to the destiny. No wonder Isaiah said WHEN I GO THROUGH THE FIRE AND THE FLOOD No one wants to go through the fire, but that is the only path for gold to become gold. It is not possible to become a victor without winning a battle. We must not give up now no matter how hard the path to that destiny maybe.

What will I tell you about David? From the moment, he was anointed and separated as the king of Israel he never had a moment of comfort, peace, and joy. It was from one battle to another; one problem to another; one conflict to another. Yet Prophet Samuel did not tell him that he would go through those travails, battles and persecution. I know that some of us are wondering why God did not foretell us these trials we are going through now. I know that David must have been confused just like you and me. There was even a time that he came back to his tents to discover that his camp had been burnt down; his wife and his soldiers' families had been taking captives and he had lost everything. Just like you and I, David wept until there was no strength in him. Have you been weeping? It is not abnormal. We have been in that state too but David did what is needed of all of us children of destiny. He encouraged himself in the Lord. He would have given up, but the fact that God who promised him the throne would never discourage him. The thought of the joy that is ahead of him encouraged him. He knew God who helped him fight Goliath is the same God that will help him out.

My friends, my own testimony is also of the fact that God has always been there for us. He was there in Ede when I could have been destroyed by my enemies; he was there at the seminary when I could have died by one of those numerous sickness; he was there with us at Abuja, always providing for our needs and I know he will always be there. That is the strength in which we must travel the race of destiny. I know that the devil will come to you to discourage you. He will tell you since you have made that mistake, your destiny has been terminated. He will tell you that since you are rejected, frustrated, poor, and lonely, your destiny has been stopped. But God asked me to tell you, DESTINY CAN'T STOP HERE.

What is that situation in your life that is about to make you give up on your destiny? What have you lost that is making you confused like all hope is gone and you can never be all that you want to be? Refuse to believe that liar (Satan). That is what he has been doing but your destiny can't stop here. "I know the pain you feel inside, and the tears you are trying to hide, but in your heart you ask God why are the words of your fellow friend on the road to destiny" Kirk Franklin. But you must remember that your promise is not equal to your problems. What you are going through now is nothing compared to the glory that will be revealed in us, says Paul (Romans 8:18). You can't afford to let your fear to bar you from your purpose. Let me announce to you that your past plus your present can never be equal to your future, if you refuse to give up.

The writer of Hebrew (Hebrew8 vs5) did not leave us in dark about what Christ Jesus went through. Although, he was the son of God, yet he learnt obedience through the things he suffered. Are you telling me Christ suffered? Yes he did. As a result, he is the author of eternal salvation, which is why he is the perfect empathizer who feels what we are feeling because he has gone through all we are going through. The writer of Hebrew went on to tell us that Christ did not consider the shame but he focused on the glory that was ahead of him (Hebrew 11vs1-3). If you therefore want to quit, why don't you join me as we look unto Jesus, the author and the finisher of our faith. What you must know is that, this is the time to shift all our attention from man to the GOD of all flesh. Men have the capacity to fail but God will not. Destiny can't stop here, it is just a matter of time no matter what you have done, and God mercy can reshape and restore you

I wonder what Isaiah saw when he said "the young shall grow weary". It means that even at a time when man is supposed to be excited and be energetically pursuing his destiny, he can become tired, weak, stumble and fall. The kind of pressure we go through sometimes is capable of breaking us down but THEY THAT WAIT UPON THE LORD WILL HAVE THEIR STRENGTH RENEWED, THEY WILL RUN AND NOT GROW WEARY, THEY WILL WALK AND NOT FAINT, THEY WILL FLY WITH WINGS LIKE EAGLE. That means it is possible not to get tired, if you run the race of destiny by the strength of your maker. There is no way a man will prevail by his own strength but when you release your all to God, he will give you the strength. Zechariah added his voice to his when he prophesized that it is not by his strength, force or human power but by the spirit of the Almighty God.

One of the reasons why many running the race of destiny will be confused, falter and be discouraged is that they are trying to reach the destiny God promised them by their strength. That is one of my mistakes. We try to fulfill God's plan plainly by human ability. Meanwhile, we have forgotten that he is a jealous God and does not share his glory with any man. That is why Isaiah says even the youth with all their strength, will stumble and fall. It is the strength of God that can carry us through the race. This is why people seek power from Satan. They seek the devil's power because they are confused and tired and they have often forgotten that the devil does not give free things? You must always remember that God is willing to strengthen you through every stage of the process. No wonder, the scripture keeps telling us that the lord was with Joseph the strength of God was available for him in the pit, in Potiphar's house and in the prison.

The strength of God will not shield you from the fire and the flood, but he will help you come out of them better. Even our Lord Jesus had to spend forty days forty nights waiting for that power that he needed for the ministry (destiny) to be fulfilled. If we must win this race, we need strength. Now that you and I are tired, I believe that is truly time for us to wait on the lord and stop waiting for men.

As I conclude, this chapter reminds us that the experience and testimony Joseph had in Potiphar's house was what helped him in the administration of Egypt's resource. David also told Goliath that the Lord that delivered him from the lion and the bear will deliver him from his hand. Your experiences now have a lot to do with your fulfillment of destiny. This is why I plead with you not to complain, rather rejoice on what God is doing in your life.

Are you truly confused, lost, and discouraged? Just remember where God is taking you to; who God is and that the Grace of God is sufficient for you. For we know that all things work together for the good of those that love the Lord and are the called according to God's purpose. You are a child of destiny, if you know where God is taking you to, then you will also know that your pains and confusions are all instrument in the hand of God to help you get there. All you need is STRENGTH from above. Recieve it now in Jesus name (AMEN).

If you decide to follow a short cut of your own;
you will be disappointed at the end.
I came to a conclusion that there
is nothing man can do to fast track Gods timing.

4 NO -NOT YET

We started the journey with great excitement that we were going to rest in this beautiful rest house that I saw on the internet. The picture I saw got stamped on my heart that each time I thought about it, I was so excited that I was taking my wife to a beautiful place to rest and spend some quality time together. Although when we left the house that morning something happened that almost made us change our minds, about the journey but what we saw kept us moving. After few hours we got to Jos, Nigeria and I was so excited that we were there after all, so we joined the vehicle that will take us to this beautiful rest house, but we never knew that the road was that bad.

The first thing that discouraged us was the vehicle that took us from the car park. This vehicle was so bad that the iron could destroy your body. As a result, the doors were not locked but we decided to keep moving. Secondly, it was when we started the journey that we discovered the road was very bad. We started wondering whether we were in the right direction. The pot holes on the road were so deep and each time we went in, my wife will complain. It was not long when I realized that my queen was so drained and when she is tired, it changes everything about her, but I started encouraging her myself that we will soon get there.

Few minutes later, when I could not bear the pains anymore I asked the driver, how far have we gone? Is the place still far? The driver assured me that we were close to the place. Meanwhile, we were not close to our destination. So, I asked again and this time it was the people that were in the vehicle that answered me, they said 'sir we are not yet there, we will soon be there'. So, each time we got to any settlement on the road I will ask them "are we there yet" and they will answer me "not yet" at a point I concluded that we were already lost, I had even forgotten how beautiful the place was, because the long journey and the bad road had removed the excitement of what I saw. I continued to ask until the people got tired of answering me. Nevertheless, I started asking myself how a beautiful rest house could be in this jungle but after few minutes, we finally arrived.

We got there and it was exactly the picture I saw on the internet.

After we finished praying, we settle down in our apartment. I asked my wife why this kind of house, so beautiful would be built in a village. Why will they do that considering that the road is bad? And as I was talking to her the Lord said to me; there is always an ugly road to a beautiful destiny.

Friends, it is possible that you are tired of praying to God for strength., you seem not to be getting any answer. This journey looks longer than you thought and now you are tired. Your family is tired and you don't even know what to say to them to keep them believing. Each time you look at the things that surrounds you the sense of guilt and sorrow overwhelms you, the path you are taking is bad and as if that is not enough, the vehicle taking you there is worse. I have a word from the Lord for you: do not give up yet; just like the people in the vehicle told me, I want you to know that you are not there yet which is why you should not give up.

Let me remind you of few things to keep you moving. Do you remember your dream? Can you remind yourself in the vision God showed you? Even if you have forgotten, do not forget what God told you. Do not forget what he says about your destiny. Do not forget the picture he showed you about your future. What the enemy is about to do is to cause you to lose sight of that glorious destiny and once you do, you will begin to go back. And the truth remains that any step you take backward slows down your journey to your destiny.

It is also imperative for me to remind you of the character of God. This God that I know is not a man that he should lie, neither the son of man that will repent. He has never broken his words; in fact He will not promise what He will not do. He does not just make promises to excite people; He always stands by His words. When there is nothing greater than to confirm His oat unto Abraham, God swore by himself. Even when the Israelites were unfaithful to him, He still ensured that they got to the promise land. Anything may change but he does not change. He is the all-knowing and all powerful, the beginning and the end. Whatever He says, He will do.

One of the problems that we have is that we want God to work with our time; we have forgotten that He is eternal and he has set time for all purpose under the heaven. You and I have to realize that there is nothing we can do to make God work in your time. He is God all by himself; He does not consult anyone before doing anything and no one can alter this decision. Solomon discovered these things when he said whatever things the lord does it shall be forever, nothing can be added to it nor removed from it, He has also set eternity in the heart of men and he does it so that all man will fear him: what a great king whose plan is indestructible. No wonder the scripture says that when the fullness of time came; he does not have abandon projects.

You know what religion has taught us is that; there is something we can do to make God do what he does not want to do. Is that not why our prayers and fasting seems to be tending towards commanding God or compelling God to do what we want. Nevertheless, there is no amount of prayer or fasting we do that can change Gods perfect plan. Many people have tried to persuade God in time past but ended up cutting their life short. You must realize that he is the one that owns your destiny. He alone can reveal it to you and He is the one who will also give you power to fulfill it. If you decide to follow a short cut of your own; you will be disappointed at the end. I came to a conclusion that there is nothing man can do to fast track Gods timing. Let me share a story with you.

As I was praying and planning to buy a car, God was planning to give me a bigger and a better car that fit the arrangement but I did not understand that, the car will be provided at the right time. I remember clearly that a brother met me when I bought the car and told me as he was praying, he warned me that I was too much in a hurry, he then went on to give me a counsel to sow that car into someone else life but I refuse to believe him or God that sent him to me, until I lost the car in a serious accident. But when the kairos time of God came, the fullness of God's time, he brought the exact car that was described to me by his servant. The lack of understanding of divine timing is one of our major problems, we sometimes feel that God is too slow on certain issues or that He is coming too late. So we devise our own method just to discover at the end that his will is perfect. Many of us are really in a hurry to do things. I have been there before but just now I understand it is not about doing something but all about doing the right thing at the right time in the right way and with the right people. I am sure that you have read the scripture that says "he makes all things beautiful in it time (Ecclesiastes chapter 3). This means that when it is not the time for that thing, it will not be beautiful. A lot of us youth want to jump the process and that is why many have met their untimely death. Check what is being built in our time, they are not built to last cause we are in a hurry. It is the fast food generation, but if you and I must arrive at our destiny we must be ready to wait for God and stick to his plan for our destiny.

Furthermore, we often give up because we are not conscious of the fact that we are closer to where we are going than before. If we remember that we are not where we are before, we are not who we are before, we will not give up. Hence the devil keeps giving us the picture that we are not making any progress. Can you honestly evaluate yourself, is this were you were before, or how you were before? NO, I am sure because you have moved, you have learnt new things. You have made progress on your journey. You have grown and you are developed. The feeling of being slow is one of those strategies the enemy of your destiny will want to use against you. Of a truth, you may not be there yet but you are on your way there. You are making progress and now you are closer to where you are going. However, if you remained where you were before, you will not make any progress. If you look carefully, you will see that you are closer to your land of promise, even if where you are is not comfortable and does not look like the promise land. Don't forget that you are on a journey and the picture is getting clearer and clearer each step you take towards your destination. So, don't to.

In addition, you must understand that it is when we are about to breakthrough we often break down. Most of the times, it is when we are close that we have the hardest hit to victory. It is when we are almost where we are going that we get tired. You are getting closer to your promised land and that is why you must not give up yet. A lot of people have thrown in the towel just a minute to their breakthrough. Some people have even turned back at that time, while some decided to try other methods but now they regret because it is now obvious to them that if they had waited a little longer, they would have seen the fulfillment of their destroyer. As I have mentioned earlier that the road to a beautiful destiny is sometimes ugly, but it is when we persevere that we get there.

In conclusion of this chapter, remember what Habakkuk says in in Habakkuk 2: 1-5, he said the vision is for appointed time, if it tarries wait for it, just ensure that you write it down; at the end it will surely reveal itself. You must see your destiny as a pregnancy which will take time before it is ripe for delivery and before that time comes; you have to patiently wait because verily, verily, I say unto you there will also be the time of delivery. This requires endurance and patience. Before the egg is hatched it must be incubated and the incubation period could be longer than you think. Nevertheless, just remember that it will surely come to pass. You can't afford to give up now!

The writer of the Epistle of Hebrews also counseled us not to throw away our confidence which has a great recompense of reward and that in a little while, He that will come will come but if anybody draws back God's soul shall have no pleasure in him; God has an undeniable future, a glorious destiny and an enviable palace for you but you must always be willing to patiently wait for the Lord. I challenge you not to seek short cuts or to withdraw from the race. A lot of people have sought shortcuts, and they have been cut short why some people have withdrawn from the pursuit of their destiny and now they are regretting. Join me as we hold-on in this journey no matter how hard the road may be. We will soon get there and when we get there you will surely forget how we got there because the joy will over shadow the pain. Let's keep moving.

If some people have risen out of deserts
and wilderness to become great
and fulfill their destiny;
then you and I have no excuse.

5

THE CLOUD OF WITNESS

Sometimes last year, a very close friend to me was involved in an accident which claimed the lives of several people who were in the vehicle with her and left her and the rest injured. Everyone in the car struggled to save themselves but at the end some made it out of the car alive while the rest died. All around us are people who are running the race-of-destiny and those who have ran and passed on.

The truth is that some were able to fulfill their destiny, they became what God created them to be and they lift for us great legacies and footprints that can guide us while some allow their destinies to be aborted and truncated. At the last solemn assembly of the Redeemed Christian Church of God, the servant of God (E.A ADEBOYE) made it clear to us that some people who fulfill their destinies (dreams and visions) became fulfilled when they were no more and they were Some who did not make it at all.

These cloud of witnesses that surround us, give testimony to several things about our pursuit to fulfill destiny. The first things I believe they are going through and the fact that the path to living a fulfilled life sometimes is ugly. I attended a funeral service recently and when we got to the cemetery I saw an inscription on one of the boards which says "we were once like you; that inscription really got me thinking. They had their own chance to fulfill destiny. They were born with a great purpose but only eternity will reveal to us if they are celebrated now.

In a soccer team, they are always about twenty two players but the coach will select eleven players who will partake in the game, while the others sit on the bench waiting for their chance and time. As the match progresses, the coach is under obligation to ensure that the players who are on the field play according to his instructions. But, when he notices that a player is not producing the desired result for the team, he brings him out and gives another player the chance and time to make his impact.

What you must realize is that whatever happens to the new player is not the fault of the coach. What am I trying to say? We must realize that some other people have been given their chance and time to fulfill their destiny, in which some of them failed to make it and were in turn substituted, some made it excellently despite the fact that all of them played in the same field. The coaching crew that worked with does that succeeded also works with those that failed. They also enjoyed the same treatments and the fans believed in all of them but they had their choice's to make. Friends, as unique as your destiny is, you must realize that some other people have walked the path you are walking.

The second thing the cloud of witnesses seem to be saying to us is that we should learn from them. 1 Corinthians 10 explains that all the Israelite's left Egypt but not all of them entered the Promised Land. Some of them were destroyed through adultery, idolatry, disobedience, pride, immorality, and their numerous sins against God, but God gave all of them equal chances. They were all baptized into Moses, they all eat the manna together, and they all saw the power of God and were all witnesses to how much God defended them. But many of them fell on the way and died, they ended up not reaching the promised destiny.

Was it God's fault that only Joshua and Caleb were able to enter it and possess the land among all those that left Egypt? No they made their choices. Paul did not hide it from us that all those things happened to them as an example for us to avoid their mistakes, so that our own destinies will not be truncated. Hence, will it not be a lamentable tragedy if we fall where they fell? Has God not been gracious enough to show us the errors of these witnesses? It is simply pathetic that many of us are still treading that same path of destruction that some of them trod.

History has afforded us the opportunity to know that, there are those major things that have destroyed a lot of destinies, which are pride, lust for power and sex. But is it not surprising that it is still this same issues that keeps destroying several people today? Our great grandfather Abraham did not escape Haggai, David did not win the battle over his sexual desires which led him to commit adultery and murder, Samson ended his great destiny on the laps of Delilah while Solomon allowed women, pride and power to destroy his promise. Yet it is still these same issues that are destroying a lot of people today even in the secular world.

Let me remind of you Tiger Woods, the one-time richest and most loved sports man in the world. How did he crumble? Recently a presidential aspirant of the United States of America was forced to withdraw because of sex scandals. What will I say about great men and women of God like Jim Baker, Jimmy Swaggart and many others that I cannot mention because of time? They all fell to the same pits. Why? It appears as if we are not hearing what the cloud of witnesses is saying.

I had the privilege of reading a book that was authored by Robert Liardon titled God's General, a book that gives account of many great men and women of God that have gone ahead of us, why they succeeded and failed. As I read this book, I discovered that the devil is still using the old trick to destroy people's destiny but in a modernized version. Hence, it was a shock to me when I realized that the author of the book himself stumbled in the same error he tried to show us. The truth is that we are not paying attention to these issues that the cloud of witnesses are showing us. Solomon in the book of proverbs and Ecclesiastes spent time to point to us the things that ruined him so that generations after him will not enter into the same errors.

The privileges and opportunities that we have now were not available to many of the heroes of faith who have gone ahead of us. Many of them never had anyone to teach them but now we have a great cloud of witnesses who had gone through most of the things that we are going through and we have their examples as a lesson to learn from. We have the word of God that contains their stories and while several generations ago, they had no access to the word of God but now we not only have access to the word of God, but to books written by great men and women of God, audio and video messages to show us the right way to lead our life. Their failure and success stories are supposed to guide us in taking our life's decisions accurately as we pursue the fulfillment of our destiny. We will be fools if we don't pay attention to these opportunities and learn.

Some of these witnesses lived their lives in a more hostile environment. Many of them had to suffer persecution and rejection in order to fulfill their destiny, yet they allowed nothing to stop them. Now they are instructing you and I to watch their errors and follow their strength but are we willing to pay attention to these things? Should you and I still allow our destinies to be aborted through sexual immoratlity, pride and power? Should we not set up measures to check ourselves?

Another crucial point that I believe that the cloud of witnesses are raising is that if they can make it to their great destiny then we also have confidence to run our own race and fulfill our destiny. One of the mistakes we make in life is that many of us have concluded that we can't win the race of destiny even before the race started. Should we not be confident that if Joseph could become what God said he will be, despite all the pains, hatred and frustration he went through? pain, hatred, and frustration should not stop you from reaching your goals.

If David can still become the greatest King in the history of Israel despite all that Saul did to him, then you have a chance to rise above your limitations. Daniel survived in Babylon and fulfilled destiny then who told you that you cannot fulfill your destiny where you are? This cloud of witnesses wants you to know that you can make it; you can rise above your limitations and reach the Promised Land.

It is important for us to choose what will be our motivation for life. So many people have chosen to see impossibilities on their path as they run the race of destiny. They know how to analyze the errors of other people and they are specialist in spreading news of people that are failing in life, thereby unconsciously accepting that they can never fulfill their own destiny. Why should you see only those that failed as examples in life? Why can't you emulate those that succeeded and build your testimony around them? If they succeeded, then what situation is telling you that you can't succeed? These people never allowed pressure and challenges of life to stop them, they fulfilled their destinies. I can imagine what they always say to themselves each time they find themselves in situations that challenged their promise; I can hear them say "my destiny can't stop here."

My friends, destiny will stop here if you allow it. You have a choice to stand in the face of any adversity and say "Yes! my destiny can't stop here." Each time Saul pursued David and he faced death, David never got tired but was always ready to fight for his destiny. As Joseph was in the pit, Potiphar's house and Prison, he never stopped talking to himself. He never allowed anything to discourage him and at last he got to his throne. As you read this book I desire that you will rise with the determination of David, Joseph, and Daniel and pursue the fulfillment of your destiny. The prison should not stop you since it did not stop Nelson Mandela, Gen Olusegun Obasanjo and several others who have risen to prominence. The difference between where you are now and where God is taking you to is TIME. It is just a matter of time, you will become all that God intends you to be; just don't give in to discouragement.

Of a truth here is a place of pain, confusion, weakness, errors, discouragement and sorrow but "there" is where you are going and you must rise above those things because destiny can't stop here. Ruth's destiny seemed to have ended in Moab; she had lost everything but she saw something that was beyond Moab and even when everyone had written her off, she kept saying to herself "my destiny can't stop here". Was that not why she followed Naomi back to Bethlehem? Yes, indeed her destiny did not stop; she got to her promised land and eventually became the great-great- grandmother to Jesus. The problem with many of us is that we often take the commas on our ways as full stop. You must see beyond here.

God is definitely not partial; he can do much more than what He did in the life of others in your life. If E.A Adeboye can rise from obscurity to become a man that the Lord has anointed and a man that has influenced the whole world in our generation; then I don't believe you should allow your destiny to stop here. Daddy G.O as he is fondly called by millions of people all over the world had no shoes to wear for the first sixteen years of his life, but that did not stop him from running the race of destiny. He rose from abject poverty to become a light in many nations; why then should you allow poverty to stop you. You and I must never forget that poverty has little to do with what you don't have but how you see yourself. I am also amazed at the great and mighty exploits that the Lord is doing through Bishop David Oyedepo knowing well how rough his journey in the ministry was. There were times when he and his family had nothing to eat but all of those things did not stop him from pursuing his call in God. Why then should you and I conclude that because we don't have what to eat and drink, then our destinies will stop here? There is more!

Time will fail me to talk about President Goodluck Jonathan of Nigeria or President Barrack Obama; how they rose from obscurity and ignored limitations on their way and become a shining star in their respective countries. Nobody would have given Obama a chance to ever becoming the president of America nor will anyone consider Goodluck Jonathan as a presidential material for Nigeria but they chose never to allow anything or anyone to stop them. When others were seeing impossibilities and difficulties on their path, they chose not to see them and eventually they got to where they were going. "Here" should not be your end; you must get "there"! If some people have risen out of deserts and wilderness to become great and fulfill their destiny; then you and I have no excuse. Who says "your destiny will stop here"? Then you must refuse to listen to them and keep fighting for your throne.

I have no doubt in my Spirit that your destiny will be fulfilled but you have to rise above limitations and fight your way out of the blockages and barriers placed on your path. It is crucial that you know that the devil does not want you to fulfill destiny. There are powers of darkness who have vowed not to let you go and become what you were born to be.

There are distractions that will come but you need to speak to yourself that if others can then you must. I will be making a big mistake if I fail to point out to you that even the Lord Jesus had reasons to quit but he fulfilled His assignment. Imagine where he came from, He was homeless, rejected and hated by people and was committed to die by crucifixion. There in the garden of Gethsemane, the Lord felt like quitting but at the end He won. If Christ went through those things, I know you may not be exonerated from going through things that will challenge your faith but you must not allow anything to stop you as you ask God for grace to move on. Christ has also shown us an example and He is the greatest witness to the fact that "destiny can't stop here". You just have to make a choice now and fight for the fulfillment of your destiny and believe in the power of God to help you to the end. If they can, yes you can and we will together fulfill our destinies.

it is crucial for us to know that what is
needed for us to fulfill our destinies
is not how we look, who we know and where we live
but our ability to effectively
use the power that is in us.

6

THE POWER THAT WORKS IN YOU

There were three different football clubs that saw him when he was a child. They all saw that he had great potentials to play football but had a major deficiency, 'his height' which is a result of a hormonal disorder. How could you commit such a huge amount of money to someone who looks like a dwarf was the question on the lips of the scouting agents of the clubs that saw him?

These scouts had to report back to the managements of their respective clubs. I can just imagine how they reported what they saw; ' oh we saw a fantastic young talented footballer but he is a dwarf and when we enquire about him we also discover he has an hormonal disorder on his growth but he is a fantastic footballer, only that he might never grow beyond his current height'. Two of the clubs immediately withdrew from this young boy and decided to go for other players that they saw. But the third club saw what the others did not see and decided to commit to bringing up this boy. They then made consultations with medical doctors and they were told that the boy had a chance of growing a little taller. Instead of giving up at that point, they went on with their commitment to bring out what they saw in the boy.

Few years later, after spending some money on this boy, he became taller and was allowed to play his first game for the club. The first thing that amazed everyone was his strength, pace and abilities to hold the ball. He held on to the ball, played with skills, ran fast with it and scored easily. There and then the club felt justified of their investments on this boy. Little did they know that this 'ElpugaAttomica' will become the finest player of the game on the planet earth? He rose out of his medical conditions and limitations and at age twenty five he has won the award of the best player on earth for four consecutive times. He did not only win several awards, broke several records and set new records. This dwarf wrote his name with gold in the history of football and has brought so many dividends for the club that believed him. I sat down one day and was considering the physique of this legend compared to his achievements and I concluded that it is because he was able to unleash the lion in him.

Friends, I know you are a child of destiny. I know that you have discovered your destiny. I'm sure you have risen above confession and frustration and I am confident of the fact that you are running the race of destiny with the faith that if others can, then you will. Also, I am persuaded that you are neither going to give up or withdraw from your pursuits no matter what happens but there is a secret I must not hide from you. This secret determines how far you will go, it determines whether you will fulfill your destiny fully or not. Several people gave up on their destiny because they did not know about it. My friends, the secret is that you must discover the power that is at work in you and unleash it.

In the pursuit of destiny, I have discovered that many of us often worry ourselves about what we don't have, that we do not pay attention to what we have. I have seen several men here and there trying to gather what they believe are the resources needed for their destiny but they have never looked inward to discover the power that is at work in them. They do not know that all that is needed to fulfill destiny is already in them. They have allowed unhealthy competition and have entered into unnecessary struggles, just because they believe someone else has what they don't have.

As I watched football and I read comments of certain people about Lionel Messi. I have often heard people say 'that boy is not a complete footballer' and I asked them why; they told me it's because of his height. Lionel Messi would be foolish to sit down and pray to be taller just because people call him an incomplete player. I was so disappointed to hear one of the football legends join them to say Messi is not a complete player because he cannot score with his head. Hence the young man has demolished a lot of big clubs with goals that came from his head. Why then would he be bothered about his height when his shortness has given him an advantage over his colleagues. His pace and strength are all due to his height. No wonder he has never replied those critics.

Dear reader, the environment where we live, the people that surrounds us and even our family members are capable of putting us under pressure. People know how to point out your weakness, they can analyze what you should have been and they have the capacity to push you to frustration, if you don't know that what you need is what God has given you no matter what you do and where you run to, you must never forget that what is on your inside is what would help you be fulfilled; not how you look. I have met people who told me that 'I wish I am like this person or the other.

How I wish I am tall? How I wish I am from this family? Stop it! That is not what should bother you. If you truly realize that you are a child of destiny and that you are uniquely created for your assignment then you will realize that you have already been made perfectly for your destiny. You have already been given all you need to fulfill destiny. What God did not give you; you should not struggle to have. He has given you all that are needed for your destiny. People who often complain about what they don't have often end up losing what they have.

I used to sometimes tell myself that if Messi had been a little bit taller than he is, maybe he would not be as fast and as strong as he is. Please stop deliberating about what you do not have when you have never used what you have.

In addition, it is crucial for us to know that what is needed for us to fulfill our destinies is not how we look, who we know and where we live but our ability to effectively use the power that is in us.. You have the grace that others do not have and that is what separates you, the real you is not how you look but what is on your inside. Is it not funny that so many people spend so much money on how to look good and not how to develop and unleash the power on their inside?

I have heard some people say I don't have anything, I am ugly, I am not intelligent but they have never paid attention to the potential on their inside. Some people cannot do maths but they are gifted in planning, yet you will hear them complain always about their inability to do maths neglecting the gift they have.

When a woman is pregnant, the husband goes to the doctor to scan to know what is inside. I do believe that we need to go to God for scan so that we will know what God has given to us and stop worrying about what God has not given us.

In marriage counseling, I have come across intending couples whose only reason for their choice of spouse is how the person looks "I love him because of he has a good height, because of his is figure". Then you ask yourself if that is enough reason to marry each other? Why will you judge a man by its container not by the content? How you look has nothing to do with whether you will fulfill destiny or not but what is in you is what matters.

Every child of destiny must seek to know what power they have been given. Power here means ability, potentials, talents and gifts. Everyone has been given the power to fulfill destiny and such destinies would never be fulfilled if we do not seek to know what we have been given and start to use it. It's one thing to know the power; it's another thing to be able to use it.

A lot of people, in a bid to compete with others have never been able to unleash the power that they have been given. Some of us have been given the power to talk convincingly while some have been given the power to sing. I will be making a mistake if I do not use my power to talk and want to sing like my friend. The truth is that the power to fulfill destiny is in you. For a long time now, we have been looking outside, looking at what we don't have but now the time has come to discover the power that God has given us.

The word of God says, "unto him who is able to do exceedingly and abundantly above all you can think of or imagine, according to the power that works in you". Your ability to do exceeding things and reach the peak depends on the power that works in you. What you should focus on is that power God has given you and how to use it. The power that works in you would help you to withstand all pressure and pain.

The power that works in you will cause you to rise above limitations and darkness. All you must do is discover it and use it. As I conclude this chapter, I want to share the story of a young man with you. This man failed at all levels in school. He kept failing untill his father and mother gave up on him and abandoned him with the grandmother. As he grew up, it was obvious that he could run but he himself never knew it. His grandmother was always impressed at the speed with which he ran errands. But one day, the coach of the athletic group of the school in the village noticed him and decided to check his speed per second.

He was surprised that this boy was better than even the best student in the school. But he had a deficiency; he was not even a student of any school because he was considered useless. The coach approached him but his fear played out instantly when he told the coach that he cannot because he was not a student. But the coach insisted he joined them only to discover that the best runner in the school was feeling envious and jealous of him but this did not distract him. He had to also put his inability to read and write aside and focus on his strength.

As time went on, the school was to be represented at the national athletics competition. The coach did not hesitate to select this boy and the former best runner. This boy got so scared that he was going to compete with the best all over the nation. Thoughts of quitting started flowing through his mind and he could not but battle with every negative word his parent had said about him, what people had told him, his lack of education and all that he had suffered in life. All of this got him distracted that he did not hear the referee's whistle to release him into the game. As a result of this, he started later than others but he spoke to himself and unleashed the power that was in him and to the amazement of everyone in the stadium, he overtook every other contestant and won.

He broke the power of failure by unleashing the power that was on his inside. What will you do my friend? To give up because of what you don't have or to set your attention on what you have so that you can be who you were made to be? All I know is that there is power on your inside which cannot be imitated or duplicated and the world would suffer in pain of it, if you refuse to unleash it. God has given us all things that pertain to life and godliness. You have it and it is time for you to rise and shine.

The peak is in you!

If your course is worth dying for,
do not relent or give up in the labour room.
Give birth to that dream
and we will celebrate you.

AN EXPECTED END

7

Le Dynamic Professeur wrote: In the labour room of dreams, hubby had not arrived. I was alone to go through the struggle. It was the 30th of May, the day our baby was born. I laid on the bed with belts strapped around my belly to monitor the baby's movement and heartbeat. I was only able to identify the faces of my gynecologist and the nurse. The contractions became intense; the worst of all, I had pains all over my body.

I was breathing so hard and was hoping that the pains wouldn't get any worse. I was then asked to start pushing. The moment I felt the contraction again, I was told to push harder. 'Take a deep breath, hold your legs, exhale, and PUSH, PUSH, PUSH!!!' that was repeated many times, almost a whole hour! It wasn't easy, I was already fully dilated yet the baby's head could not be seen. For a whole hour, that was what I did, Push. I just wanted to get my baby out as soon as possible . . . after a while, it came out. At 3pm on the dot of time, the final push was done and out slided our bouncing baby boy.

There are four things that could happen in such situations. First, the mother and the baby makes it alive out of the labour room, second the mother might die and the baby makes it out alive, third baby might die and the mother surviving the labour room experience and lastly both the mother and baby might die in the labour room.

Hmmm . . . in the labour room of dreams, some dream beavers make it alive with their dreams while some die in the labour room of their dreams but their dreams didn't die with them, their dreams lived on in their stead. Some gave up and their dreams died in the labour room and they came out empty handed.

I am sure no one wants to either die with his/her dreams unborn or make it out of the labour room empty. The beauty of the labour room is for the BABY to be BORN. No one wants to come out of the labour room EMPTY. Some people even though died in the labour rooms of their dreams, they died pushing. They labored for something worth more than their lives and the whole world celebrates them till today. People like Martin Luther King Jnr, found a course to die for and he lived and died for it. AWESOME! If your course is worth dying for, do not relent or give up in the labour room. Give birth to that dream and we will celebrate you.

Maybe your dream is not a course to die for. Perhaps yours is one you would have to live to see it come alive. I urge you today, do not give up PUSHING, PUSH! PUSH!! PUSH!!! Are the contractions becoming more intense? Are the pains becoming more unbearable? Is it beginning to look like you can't make it beyond where you are right now? It is part of the labour room process. Do not be scared if you go through it alone. Still don't give up if your parents, husband, boyfriend or girlfriend leaves you to it. The dream is yours and yours to bear. You must give birth to it.

Circumstances may be hard. You may experience so much pain in every facet of life. Your school fees may be so difficult to pay; it is possible that debts are about swallowing you up. Right now your peers may have gone far ahead of you. Your parents may have even disowned you because of your dreams. It is very possible that your friends are always mocking you. Listen! When you are going through tough times, take a deep breath, when it seems as if you can't go on anymore, I tell you, it's time to hold your legs and PUSH! Yes, that's what happens in the labour room. It is never a pleasant experience. But the BEAUTY of it is making it out of there with that BABY in your hands. Do not give up my friend; you are in the labour room of your dreams . . . PUSH and PUSH REAL HARD.

.

My dear friend, the greatest desire of the almighty God is for your destiny to be fulfilled. He wants you to give birth to your dream. The one that creates thinks of nothing than for you to get to the destination he created you to get to. He has an end in mind for you even before you were born and it will be a disaster if you do not reach there. God said through Jeremiah that 'I know the thoughts I have towards you, the thought of good and not evil, to give you an expected end' it has never been the desire of God for any of his children's destiny to be aborted.

He is a loving father whose concern is to see all of his children fulfill their dreams. He doesn't want your dreams to die in you nor for you to die without seeing the manifestation of your destiny but he has left us with a choice.

You may want to know why some people did not reach the expected end; why some people died in the labour room. Some made it but their destinies got truncated and you will want to know why. First and foremost, we must realize that God does not break his word. It was not God's fault that most of the Israelites did not enter the promise land. I remember my pastor once told me that the fact that God said a man will be great does not automatically guarantee the person's greatness. God has a part to play and he is always faithful to his words. You can be sure that what he says, he will do, he will surely do but what if the person involved stands against his own destiny.

According to God's plan, he pronounced that the family of Eli will stand as priest forever in his temple but Eli and his children truncated that plan by their frivolous living. God always seeks to bring us to the expected end but he will not force us. Rather he will daily instruct us on the path to follow. Hence we have to make the choice to either obey him or not. What do you think will happen to a pregnant woman who refuses to heed to the warnings and instructions of the doctor on how to keep the pregnancy safe and fit for delivery?

The doctor's interest is for her to give birth safely and for her to also come out alive but if the woman refuses to heed all the warnings, then she will have herself to blame. God is always faithful but we humans are always bent on following our own way. Friends, you need to know that God has always stood by his word. When he says I will make you into a great nation, he means it and he is ready to put all it takes in motion to bring that to pass but what if the person involved refuses to follow the path that will see the promise come to pass? God can be trusted. You have to make up your mind that you will not be the one that will destroy the plan of God for your life. There are various distractions that you will encounter on your path; you just have to make up your mind that they will not stop you from fulfilling your destiny.

If truly, you have come to discover your worth, your mission on earth and the fact that you are on course even though the path you are threading is thorny, then you should make up your mind to make it count. Decide to be all you were created to be. Fight if need be, discipline yourself, let your eyes be fixed on the joy that is ahead. Let the fulfillment of your destiny be your motivating factor, let it motivate you to go through the labour room without complaining. The glory that is ahead should make you endure the gory path you are threading now.

The joy of delivery often overwhelms the heart that it makes us forget the pain of the labour room. But what is the essence of the pains if the baby will not come out alive or if the mother will not live to carry the baby. The end should matter to you than the beginning and the path you take now. That is why the man of God- Moses was grieved with the Israelites because they were not conscious of their end. What justifies the means is the end of the journey. My greatest prayer for you is to finish your race well and fulfill your destiny but the choice is yours to make. Will you be ready to follow the path that your maker has identified for you to fulfill your destiny or will you follow your path? Of a truth, the lord desires that you see the fulfillment of your destiny but you have a role to play. I hope you have no forgotten that it is he that endures to the end that will be saved.

In conclusion, your destiny can't end here. If you will not give up in you labour room, you will surely see the manifestation of God's glory in your life. Do not lose sight of God's purpose for your life even in your pains. Remember that here is not the ultimate so don't become slaves of the immediate. Don't allow the pleasure of the now or the pressure you face now to stop your destiny. You are more than 'here'. I may not know what here stands for in your life but just remember that there is an expected end God had in mind for you before you were born and that should be the ultimate. If you must sacrifice anything, don't sacrifice your future just to be satisfied now. Why not sacrifice the pains and the present pleasure to reap the future. It is up to you if you will allow your destiny to be aborted here. As for me, I have my mind to continue to PUSH, PUSH and PUSH until I have my baby. I will not allow anybody to pull me out of my purpose. I will rather hold on to see my baby than to quit and lose what I have been suffering for.

I have been insulted, assaulted and maltreated, misunderstood. Rejected, dejected, abused, talked about, ridiculed and reproached but all of those things will not stop my destiny. I know the devil is afraid of what I will become later and that is why he is trying to stop me down. But I refuse to give up to that lie. My destiny can't stop here. Paul was in my shoes, when he said we are hard-pressed on every side but not crushed, we are perplexed but not in despair, persecuted but not forsaken, struck down but not destroyed, for our light affliction which is for a moment is working for us a far more exceeding and eternal weight of glory (2 Corinthians 4:8-9, 17). That is why nothing will make us to stop until we reach the destination God has in mind.

Let me just remind you of how glorious the end will be. You need to have a picture of what God's destiny for your life is. You need to just picture how beautiful your life and will be. Christ Jesus set the joy above the curse. You must be able to say I know where God is taking me to; I know his plan for me is beautiful. I know that when we get there, everyone will understand why I subjected myself to that painful process.

The expected end God showed you should keep you moving. Don't stop here. Keep pursuing what you see. No matter how bad the road may be, in the fullness of time, your life will speak for itself.

DON'T FORGET THIS

'If you must sacrifice anything, don't sacrifice your future just to be satisfied now. Why not sacrifice the pains and the present pleasure to reap the future. It is up to you if you will allow your destiny to be aborted here.'

No matter how disappointed you are,
don't give up, find another route.
What matters most is for you
to get to where God want you to be,
so don't get depressed if you meet that road block.

THE FINAL WORD

As we jet out of Nigeria on July 13th, 2015, one of our silent hopes was that now we will be in a place where there will be no struggle and we can finally fulfil God's purpose for our life. This was because we knew that our coming to the United States was not born out of our own personal ambition to live in the United States but was born out of a definitive instruction that the Lord gave us and revealed to us since 2005. But, what we did not know was that coming to the United States of America is not the same thing as fulfilling our destiny. Therefore, we were mistaken to think that everything will become easy and smooth, but we did not realize that the brighter your light, the thicker the darkness that surrounds it. Yes, we had forgotten that each new level brings us face to face with another battle to fight, another mountain to climb and another river to cross as we pursuit our destiny. It suddenly occurred to us when we got here that we have not attained anything, rather it was time to forget the past and press on to fulfil the purpose why God has opened the door of North America to us. My wife and I knew that if it was not the Lord that purposed our coming, we will not be able to come considering our situation. As at the time God first spoke to me about coming to the United States of America to serve his purpose, I had no idea of how it was going to come to pass but I decided to make the first attempt of applying to come to school here in 2005, but each time I got to the point of finances and sponsorship, I abandoned the application. In 2007, 2008, 2009 and 2012 I attempted coming to the United States and gave up on it because I thought within myself that there was no way I can afford the expenses. But, I knew that God spoke to me that he has an assignment for me in the United States and I continue to dream that I was given visa to come to the United States but each time I had the dream, I missed my flight in the dream.

Therefore, in 2015 when God finally opened the door and brought us to America, I knew it was for preaching the Gospel and planting churches because in each of the dreams that I had before coming here, I saw myself looking for land to plant and pioneer a new church. Hence, our assumptions were that if God brought us here, everything will come easy and we will not have to struggle for anything. Yes, we came with the sense that the journey to fulfilling destiny will be easy moving forward, but we failed to remember that until we stand before the Lord in the end of journey and He says "well-done, my good and faithful servant" we cannot stop. How then can we start celebrating when the journey is not yet over? It is easy for us to assume that we have arrived because we have come to a place of comfort but only a fool will assume that achievements and fulfilments are the same. More so, what many of us will call achievements is not recognized by the Lord. One story that illustrates this point so well was the story of the disciples returning to Jesus with joy and the testimony that even demons were submitting to them but in the eye of Jesus, that was not the achievement to celebrate, their joy should come from the fact that their names were written in the book of life (Luke 10:20). Our destiny was not just about traveling to America or living in America, as great as living in America or becoming an American citizen may be, the only joy that should fill our heart is that we are daily in the center of the will of God as we daily live our lives to fulfil the purpose for which we were sent to the world.

Paul the Apostle was a man of great understanding who recounted his exploits in his epistle written to the Philippians but as great as those exploits were, he constantly reminded himself that he had not attained glory, therefore there was no need for premature celebration. Hear what he said "Brothers and sisters, I do not consider myself yet to have taken hold of it.

But one thing I do: Forgetting what is behind and straining toward what is ahead, I press on toward the goal to win the prize for which God has called me heavenward in Christ Jesus. Philippians 3:14". It was that understanding that helped Apostle Paul to move forward even when his past successes and pain could have deterred him from making progress. The Apostle realized that his ultimate success was to win the prize of the high calling, therefore, he must continue to daily press on. It did not take long for us to realize that same truth when we got to the United States. We discovered that every day of our journey, we must keep fighting, keep pressing, keep praying, keep trusting and keep believing. The goal is to win the prize for which the Lord Jesus called us, the goal was to finish the assignment that we were sent to accomplish and that means that the devil will continue to attack us, our faith will be tried and we will always get to that point of wanting to give up but we cannot afford to faint until we win.

It was not long after we arrived in the United States that the Lord instructed us to move to Maryland. Most of the people who knew us questioned my sense of reasoning, but my wife and I reached a conclusion when we got married that whenever God speaks to us, we don't argue or consider how sensible that instruction may sound because we know for sure that we are on a journey that he created us for and our opinion or feelings does not matter. Some people tried to persuade us to stay put but we were certain it was God. Therefore, I put in a transfer request to move to Maryland and it was approved. We moved not knowing what the plan was, and since we don't have anyone really in Maryland, we contacted someone that we knew and pleaded with him to take us in so that in return I can serve with him in the church. This great man of God agreed but it was not long that we discovered that it was not part of God's plan for us, so we became homeless; but the Lord who told us to come to Maryland had His own plans and He provided accommodation for us through a church in Maryland where I started serving as a volunteer preacher as the church awaited the arrival of the Pastor that was hired from Nigeria. Indeed, that was the plan, it began to unfold as the Lord himself had arranged it. The pastor we intended to be with at first, thought that we had planned what happened, he felt offended, angry and bitter but he did not know that we came to the United States with just one thing; "a word from the Lord".

Therefore, we pressed on with the decision never to step outside the plan of God. I know you want to know how easy it was for us to do that; the simple answer is that it was never easy. It was filled with pain, hunger and hatred from the people we relied on, but we stuck to the plan that God was unfolding right in our own eyes. We had no idea that there was a church who will need us to fill a temporary void, but God knew, and it was all about him. Hence, as everything was unfolding, the human nature kicked in at the time we were feeling very comfortable in this church, which reminded us why we were in the United States in the first place. Thus, I reached out to the North American Missions Board to share with them the vision of church planting that the Lord laid on my heart from Nigeria and we were accepted to be part of the missionaries with NAMB after we were assessed. The excitement of what NAMB was going to provide in support of the vision of planting a church quickly clouded our sight and we shifted focus from the Lord who sent us here to this organization. We failed to always remember that it is all about the Lord and not about anyone else.

A year, seven months after we started serving with this church, the Lord made it clear that our time was up, and it was obvious because we became so uncomfortable at the church. Thus, we decided to pursue planting the church that God instructed us to plan from Nigeria, but we started on the wrong foundation which was depending on NAMB and the people that promised to be part of the new church. Obviously, they failed and we were let down by everyone around us. It was at this point that we thought that we should abandon church planting, since everyone has failed us and the church planting was not coming along as we thought. But as we were contemplating on what to do, the Lord reminded me about this book which He inspired me to start writing in the year 2013 when the heat of running the race of destiny was so immense and all we could think of was giving up and throwing in the towel. As I began to read through this manuscript, I could hear God saying loudly to us, "You can't just stop here".

My friend, the journey continues, the battle is not yet over, it is still fierce and tiring, but there is no quitting, there is no stopping, not now or later, the only time to rest is when we see the savior and He says well-done. Even as I write this final chapter, the only assurance that we have is that our destiny is secured in Christ Jesus and if we are at the center of his will, there is no giving up. There are times when giving up seems to be the only option, but you and I must be at that point when our comfort is sacrificed for God's will.

You and I must trust God for courage to move on even when it seems as if we have failed. When we fail, it is not God's plan that failed, we are often the reason for failure. God only must be trusted, His plans only must be followed, but even in our place of error, his mercy is the only way out and it is in trusting his mercy that you can find strength to move on. Hear what Paul said "therefore, since through God's mercy we have this ministry, we do not lose heart (2Corinthians 4:1)." Paul did not give up despite the several pains, trials, beatings, maltreatment, abuse and rejection he went through, even when his life was in danger or peril. Why? God's mercy.

The mercy of the Lord is all that can sustain us in that moment when all hell seems to have broken loose and it seems that there is no where to go. His help is all we need when we are so vulnerable, and failure is staring us in the face. We can depend on his mercy when our best friends turn against us, betray us and our journey is all rough. Only God's hand of love and grace can sustain us after we have tried everything but failed. It is disheartening and heartbreaking to be written off but when it happens, only the everlasting arm can carry you through. As Jesus Christ our Lord and Savior was betrayed by one of his disciples, denied by his best pal, abandoned by his trusted followers, you and I can only depend the unchanging love and mercy of the father when we face such situation. Do you remember that Jesus our Lord and savior took his disciples to the garden of gethsemane where he went to pray, requesting them to pray for him? Did they pray for him? No! They slept! My friends, you and I will come to such moments when our prayer partners will not care about us and we will be left all alone to go through that moment, yet, the mercy of God will sustain us.

Dear brothers and sisters, you cannot afford to give up! You cannot afford to throw in the towel! It is true that everything around you make you feel like a failure, but your identity is not in what you do, your identity is in who you are in God. The SEND city coordinator for NAMB never even believed in me, he did not give me a chance, I remembered he said to me shortly after I passed the assessment "we cannot invest in you because we don't believe that you will succeed". Of a truth he starved me of all the support that we needed for the church planting and when the church planting hit the rock, you can imagine the sense of failure that overtook me and overwhelmed me. But my wife constantly reminded me that I have not failed. One night, as I was driving back home from school, the road that I was traveling on suddenly ended because of some repair going on, so I had to find another route to get home.

As I got home, the Holy Spirit said to me "it is possible that the road you are traveling on is closed, but it does not mean that your journey has ended; all you need to do is find another route by asking the Lord what other route he had made available for you". That night when the main road I wanted to take was closed, I checked my navigating app to find another route. There are times your road is close, but it does not mean that you have come to the end of the road. Just pray and ask the Holy Spirit for another route. It is often painful to start all over, but it is better to start over than to give up. No matter how disappointed you are, don't give up, find another route. What matters most is for you to get to where God want you to be, so don't get depressed if you meet that road block. Many of our friends gave up when they almost got to their destination, many have committed suicide because they did not get to where they wanted through, the way they hoped to get there but my friend, it's not about you. It is not about where you want to get to in life, it is not about your dream, it is all about what God want to do with your life, so don't judge your life by the standard of men. Keep moving!

Finally, you must remember that the goal is not to get the applause of men or reach the heights that you have set for yourself, the goal is for you to fulfil your destiny. Nobody will doubt the success of Paul at that time when he wrote Philippians because he had planted several churches and he was imprisoned at this time, but he knew that the prize to be won is from the Lord and not from men. The applause of men means nothing to him until the Lord himself applauds him. His ultimate prize was not an award of excellence from men or recognition but the only prize that Jesus will give to all his faithful servants.

If you make reaching the standard that people set for you your goal, the applause of men, awards from people and rewards in material things of life, you will lose focus and get depressed whenever people tell you that you are a failure, which is why pleasing the Lord who sent you into this world on a mission is the only goal you must pursue. Your destiny is not a certificate to acquire, a house to buy, a car to drive, an achievement to applaud by people, you were destined to bring God glory by fulfilling the mission for which he sent you to the world and there is only one voice you must be eager to hear, at the end of your days on earth and it should be the voice of your creator saying to you, well-done. Therefore, don't get depressed or be sad if people do not appreciate you, reward you, award you or recognize what you are doing, the only one who can judge you successful is the one who made you and sent you here and until he says you are successful, you are not. Therefore, you cannot give up until you finish your race. Paul reminded us that it is not everyone that runs in a race that will win, so, you must run your own race to win. What is the essence of running a race without victory in mind?

Winning your race is what should keep you moving no matter what you face on the way. If you fall, get up, don't just quit your race. Don't run with the mind of impressing people, run with the mind of winning for the one who put you in the race. There is no competition between you and others, your race was set before you by your creator to be run by you with the mind of completing it not minding when others finish theirs or how glorious their own race was run. It is time to stay focused on winning your race. As I have said in the previous chapters, for you to run your race to the finish line, there is no giving up. The Lord Jesus set his eyes on the glory ahead which was why He refused to be distracted by the pain of the cross. My friends, there is joy ahead, I mean the joy of sharing in God's glory eternally; therefore, you can't just stop here. Until you become all that God created you to be and you fulfill all that He sent you to the world to do, there is no stopping, no quitting and no throwing in the towel. Therefore, say with me with boldness "I just can't stop here".

OTHER BOOKS WRITTEN BY
REV ADEREMI BADRU

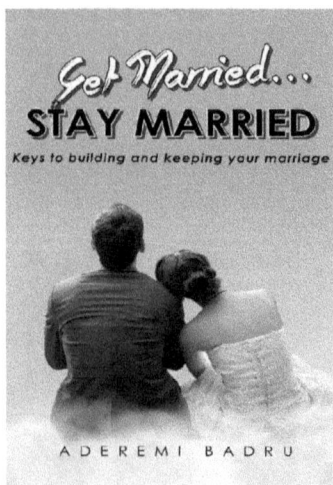

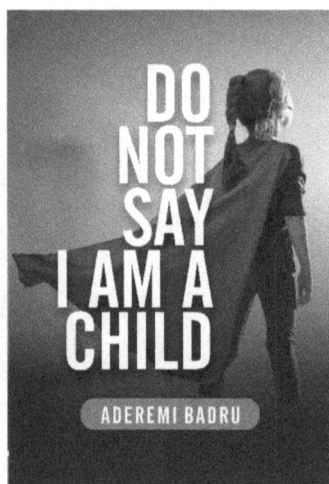